—— THE INCIDENTS

POST-HUMAN KNOWLEDGE & THE CRITICAL POST-HUMANITIES

by ROSI BRAIDOTTI

———— March 12, 2019
Piper Auditorium, Gund Hall
Harvard University
Graduate School of Design
Cambridge, Massachusetts, USA

Introduced by John May ———— Organized by the Master
in Design Studies Program and Womxn in Design ————
Produced by Ken Stewart, Paige K. Johnston, and Patric Verrone
———— Published by Harvard Design Press and Sternberg Press

JOHN MAY: My name is John May, the Director of the MDes program here at Harvard but also the Area Head of the History and Philosophy of Design and Media Group, who is cohosting this event with the Graduate School of Design (GSD) Womxn in Design project. And I want to thank them all for cohosting Rosi Braidotti's visit and the event this morning. I am honored to welcome Rosi Braidotti to the GSD. It's no exaggeration to describe Rosi as one of the most important living philosophers and a central international figure in feminist and posthumanist thought. Her intellectual project sits at the convergence of some of the most difficult conditions of our time, asking questions that cut across all of lived life—questions of gender and sexuality; of technology and materiality; of politics, power, and marginalization; and, increasingly, of ethics and the earth. ——— The past year has been an emotional one in the design fields, perhaps nowhere more so than at the GSD. And as we reckon with a troubling history of institutionalized gender discrimination and frequent misogyny, we are also dealing with an equally troubling persistence of those realities in the present. When this reckoning began, I felt it could be meaningful to place these issues in a broader intellectual framework, to ask of their relationship to the history of Western humanism, and to the Enlightenment and liberalism more generally—these long, unfolding cultural projects that have produced both good and evil in our time. Rosi Braidotti's was the first name that came to mind when I tried to imagine who was best able to help us in this project. —————— At a moment when our political culture is completely defined by deepening anti-intellectualism, it seems important now to reaffirm the basic principle that our complex social realities require an intellectual engagement commensurate with those complexities. That engagement takes hard work, and patience, and commit-ment, and energy. These are qualities that have defined Rosi's life. —————— Rosi Braidotti is Distinguished University Professor Emerita at Utrecht University and founding director of the Centre for Humanities at Utrecht. She was the founding professor of the Women's Studies program at Utrecht in 1988, established the first official PhD program in Women's and Gender Studies, and, for seventeen years, directed the Utrecht Women's Studies Center—a center whose enrolled student cohort now numbers in the hundreds. She helped establish and later directed, for ten years, the Athena Network, an extensive community of European scholars and activists committed to women's studies that included, at its height, over 130 member institutions all over the European Union. And in 2010, the Athena Network was awarded with the Erasmus Prize for its outstanding contributions to fostering social inclusion through education. Rosi has been invited to teach at the top universities in the world, and also delivered the Tanner Lectures on Human Values at Yale in 2017. ——— Rosi was born in Italy and grew up in Australia, where she received a first class honors degree from the Australian National University in Canberra in 1977 and was awarded the University Medal in Philosophy. She then moved on to do her doctoral work at the Sorbonne where she received her degree *cum laude* in philosophy in 1981. Braidotti's publications have consistently been situated in continental philosophy at the intersection of social and political theory, cultural politics, gender and feminist theory, race and ethnicity studies, and posthumanism. Throughout her work, she asserts and demonstrates the importance of combining theoretical concerns with a serious commitment to producing socially and politically relevant scholarship that contributes to making a difference in the world. Together with her partner Anneke Smelik she set up the Rosanna Fund for Women at Utrecht University to support women's scientific and academic careers. So please join me in welcoming Rosi Braidotti.

AUDIENCE: [*Applause*]

ROSI BRAIDOTTI: I am very touched by that generous introduction by John May: thank you. It is a great pleasure, and a great honor to be here. I have so many dear old friends here at Harvard: Alice Jardine and I were at graduate school together in the days when everybody was in Paris. And it is lovely to see Verena Conley, one of the pioneers of Deleuze studies in the days when people did not seem to care much for neo-materialism. Thank you all for being here. ——— Well, I only have fifty minutes to try to outline the challenges of the posthuman condition, so I'll try to use the time wisely and to my best advantage. Posthuman philosophy raises so many issues of method and meta-methodology that it inevitably leaves some of them unexplored. This is one of the reasons I favor a cartographic philosophical method, which traces road maps without attempting to be exhaustive. What this means for my interlocutors, you the audience, is that you can annotate those road maps yourselves as we go along, and then we can return to them as open questions in the discussion if you wish. It is a materially grounded collective practice. ——— My presentation mixes the critical and the creative voices. What I would like to do is to evoke a number of critical concerns around the state of what counts as *the human* today, and how that affects social relations, theory, design practices, and the academic humanities But I also want to adopt a very affirmative approach and a constructive outlook about the great potential of the posthuman theoretical framework. I will argue that the new field of the Critical Posthumanities is growing fast and making a significant impact on the academy. These new fields of knowledge production should make us dream and hope for the future. ——— Let me start by outlining some key assumptions. Firstly, thinking about *the human* and questioning what counts as *the human* is not something that humanists do.

Or rather, humanists talk about humans as linguistic entities, social units, polities, as cultural entities within political organizations. And we in the academic humanities are happy to leave the detailed discussions as to what actually defines *the human* to anthropologists, biologists, and those people who are the specialists of "life." This paradox is built into the humanities, where *the human* conventionally falls into patterns of dualistic oppositions that define it by what it is not. ——— Secondly, *the human* is equated with Man—more specifically, the Renaissance ideal of the Vitruvian Man, revived in the European Enlightenment as the "measure of all things." And that universal Man is sure not a woman, is not an African, is not an animal, is not nature, is not a robot. It is *not*. And it is this definition by negation that begs the question of what actually *is* our consensus about being human, and what counts as the point of reference—the basic unit—by which we would define the human. Discussions about the human are currently on a roll: amuse yourselves, as you are the designers and architects, and have a look at how many festivals of *the human* and festivals of the humanities are taking place in the cities of the world, from Dubai to Melbourne to London. Entire cities are seemingly going out of their way to try to festivalize the idea that we have no conceptual rigor about being *human* in today's world. What used to be an axiom has become a playground. ——— I refer to this relocation of *the human* in terms of the posthuman convergence, which I will try to define for you briefly. As an event, it forces us to confront the paradoxes, aporias, and the little big denials that we have developed, as humanists, around the notion of *the human*. ——— I have defined the posthuman as our historical condition, and not some future dystopia (Braidotti, 2013). Furthermore, I approach the posthuman as an affirmative condition, not as a terminal crisis. The posthuman condition is the convergence, across the spectrum of cognitive capitalism, of post-humanism on the one hand and post-anthropocentrism on the other. The former focuses on the critique of the humanist Eurocentric ideal of "Man" as the alleged universal standard, while the latter criticizes species hierarchy and human exceptionalism. ——— Equally interdisciplinary in character, they are linked to separate social movements and to different theoretical and disciplinary histories that do not necessarily follow from each other. You can be critical of Western humanism and remain perfectly anthropocentric, or critique anthropocentrism but cling to humanistic values. Their intersection is therefore a bit of a clash, not a harmonious synthesis. It is currently producing a chain of theoretical, social, and political effects and a qualitative leap in new conceptual directions, which I call the Critical Posthumanities (Braidotti, 2019). ——— Of course, if you come from the radical epistemologies—my political families of feminism and anti-racism or anti-fascism—you will already have an open quarrel with the ontology of *the human*. And if you come from the critical philosophical traditions, then you will know that *the human* is anything but a neutral term, and that Man is defined as much by what he includes in his definition of his humanity as by what he excludes. Not only is this Man not universal, but it is a culture-specific construct. And it is a term, *the human*, that indexes access to entitlements, visibility, and power. ——— To be human enough, or *not* human enough, is assessed in terms of conforming to the dominant standard and norm, that is to say the degrees of similarity to that particular design of Man. The human is therefore indexed to power relations, which makes it anything but neutral. The historical moment that I define as the *posthuman condition* brings all these tensions to the fore. My argument is that feminist, decolonial, race, and Indigenous theories are of the utmost relevance in approaching this issue (Braidotti, 2022). ——— I chose to describe the predicament that we are in as a *convergence*, that is to say as an intersection and merging of diverse events. The term *posthuman* itself is very heterogeneous, so let me proceed in order and describe my notion of the posthuman as a convergence phenomenon, starting from the conceptual intersection of critiques of the humanistic tradition on the one hand and critiques of anthropocentrism on the other.

Post-Humanism, Post-Anthropocentrism, and the Posthuman

The scholarship on humanism is enormous and depending on which theoretical, political, or ethical tradition you were trained in, you may think that one may follow necessarily from the other, so that critiquing humanism entails exposing anthropocentrism. This, however, is not always or necessarily the case. Derrida (2008) defends that argument, as if undoing humanism would always allow anthropocentrism to come to the fore. But if you look at the empirical reality of the scholarship on the posthuman, that does not bear to the evidence. The two lines of inquiry often run parallel and ignore each other. ——— A very strong tradition of critiques of humanism begins as far back as the eighteenth century, following the Universal Declaration of Human Rights with the French Revolution in 1792. Almost immediately, a woman by the name of Olympe de Gouges pointed out that the Universal Declaration of Human Rights only applied to free men, native of their country. To strike a better and more equal balance, Gouges wrote the alternative: a Universal Declaration of Women's Rights (1791). And I suppose you know what happened to the heroic Olympe de Gouges? She was sent to the guillotine immediately, by her revolutionary "brothers," who evidently had no time to waste on matters such as sex or gender equality. ——— Furthermore, in 1792—in the middle of the French Revolution, speaking of the Universal Declaration of Human Rights—the antislavery activist Toussaint Louverture raised pertinent questions: Do universal human rights apply to the enslaved people? Aren't they humans, too? About a century later, abolitionist Sojourner Truth would address the same exact topic to the activists of the First Feminist Wave: Do Rights for Women also apply to Black women? Aren't they humans too? In 1794, Toussaint Louverture led the Haitian Revolution, liberated all the slaves, and established a free democratic republic on the basis of the principles of the French Revolution. But then what happened to Toussaint Louverture? The French Imperial Army got involved, squashed the liberation movement—downgraded to the status of a race rebellion—and sent him into captivity. ——— My point is that both historically and conceptually the critique of humanism is simultaneous and absolutely coextensive with humanism itself. A point that Edward Said was to make later (2004), to explain the great longevity of humanism: it produces and absorbs its own modes of critique. By extension, criticism of the universal idea of Man has always already been present. And this is, I repeat, the strength as well as the weakness of humanism. But where does it leave the critique of anthropocentrism? ——— The novelty of the current situation is both the co-occurrence of the two critiques—of humanism and of anthropocentrism—and their extreme urgency. The focus is especially on the specificity and the complexity of the issues around anthropocentrism— that is to say, species supremacy, because they are new to the humanists' agenda. The idea that we humans are a species— *anthropos*—that has aggressively granted ourselves the right to access, use, and exploit every body and every organism that lives is not a common notion. It is rather an uncomfortable truth that stresses human aggression and our collective ability to deny the autonomy of other species. Even more importantly, it also disavows the interdependence between humans and the other species that feed and support us. ——— The critique of species supremacy and human exceptionalism is distinct from that of the other sociological variables—class, ethnicity, gender and sexuality, race, religion, disability, etc. These lines of critique can run parallel to each other without ever intersecting. They do not necessarily intertwine until they are literally thrown together in the posthuman convergence that we now find ourselves in. ——— The posthuman convergence is consequently a set of crossovers. It's a series of interrelations, not a linear phenomenon—very rhizomatic, it unfolds into one thousand plateaus of nomadic phenomena. It is a zigzagging pattern of resonating causes and issues carried by the two fundamental events that structure our historicity: on the one hand, the Fourth Industrial Revolution (Schwab, 2015), the knowledge economy, also known as cognitive capitalism. And, on the other hand, the Sixth Extinction (Kolbert, 2014), also known as the climate change crisis and the dying of the species, that threatens our planetary survival. ——— These events are happening simultaneously. It's not as if we have climate change on Monday and AI and synthetic biology on Tuesday. They are happening at the same time. How to think the simultaneity of boom-and-bust on this scale, or as a multiscalar or multidimensional event, is what the posthuman challenge entails. It is not helpful to set up new separations between discursive fields, as it does not help construct the transdisciplinary task force we need in order to address the complexity of issues confronting us in the posthuman predicament. ——— Some may say that maybe all this has happened before in history, but I doubt it because no methodology or protocol has been handed down through the ages to support the effort to think about the implosion of the human. Critical posthuman consciousness is certainly causing a great deal of panic but also, as we will see in a minute, incredible excitement about the future. These are really the best of times and the worst of times. ——— To think such dissonance (Braidotti, 1991), such intensive nomadic shifts (Braidotti, 1994; 2011a; 2011b), however, demands skills of endurance, of imagination, and of transversal connectivity.

Transversality is really the key term here. You need to draw a line across events that are not at all similar or parallel even— learn to function by transpositions (Braidotti, 2006). *Trans*. The future is in the *transversality* of almost everything.

Thus, the first step of the argument I want to make is that we now need to explore these two intersecting phenomena—post-humanism and post-anthropocentrism—together and apart, in a systemic manner. We have to look at the chain of theoretical, social, and political effects they trigger and try to steer a course that would allow us to have something productive, affirmative, and propositional to offer. I want to qualify immediately, however, my use of the pronoun "we." Who are "we"? The term points firstly to a philosophical tradition— that of my French teachers who made anti-humanism into a respectable set of ideas: Foucault, Irigaray, and Deleuze especially. As a continental philosopher located in Europe, my work is situated in this lineage of materialist life philosophy of immanence, difference, and heterogeneity (Braidotti, 2017).
——— Secondly, it applies to a careful analysis of the power relations it enlists in its very enunciation. "We," the category we, like all categories, is not unitary. And we is not One. "We" needs to be put carefully in inverted commas, grounded according to the politics of immanence, or in the feminist variable—the politics of location (Rich, 1984). Being embodied and embedded means we all speak from somewhere, in both space and time. "We" have multiple critical genealogies— we may come from feminism and LGBTQ+ politics, from anti-racism, from anti-fascism, from environmental and media activism—the list is open. But the rule is the same: be grounded, but keep flowing. By extension: be accountable for a specific slice of lived experience, a location grounded in class, age, gender, sexuality, race awareness, and Indigenous epistemology, as a specific perspective (Braidotti and Bignall, 2018).
——— All of these locations are ways in which you can ground

your statements, expressing a critique of universalism without falling into relativism. The opposite of universalism is not relativism. The opposite of universalism is perspectivism: multiple, grounded perspectives. ———— The posthuman predicament confronts us with a fundamental tension: "we" may well be confronting the threats and challenges of the third millennium, together, but "we" are not One, or the Same—we are differently positioned in terms of power, entitlement, and access of the very conditions that define us. "We" are not a homogeneous notion but a complex and diverse one, which reflects the multiple differences that compose "us." But it is nonetheless the case that "we" are in the posthuman convergence together.

I argued above that we, the human and nonhuman inhabitants of this particular planet, are currently positioned between the Fourth Industrial Revolution and the Sixth Extinction. This two-pronged convergence of advanced technology with even more advanced environmental degradation calls for an extra effort of representation: How do we bring the digital and the ecological into dialogue with one another? Think for instance of the role of AI in providing supportive, caring robots that will take a great deal of hard work and drudgery away from the humans. But then expand the argument to think also about unmanned warfare and killer drones, and the picture becomes immediately more complex. ——— The power relations between the different branches of the posthuman convergence are uneven. The digital domain does rule in our world; however, it is also the case that the environmental cost of these technologies is excessive, both in terms of their production and of their disposal. These two dimensions are not at all equal in political weight. Relevant research on digital waste drives the point home (Gabrys, 2011). You will even have trouble finding images of digital garbage on the internet, because Apple and the other tech giants make sure that the only images of rubbish you see are organic. An electronic device—in particular a branded one, like a dirty old Apple computer—being dismembered by the same people who made them in some faraway land, with the lithium batteries exposed and all their toxic elements pouring out, is not a desirable image. You will not find many of those. ——— And yet, we need to think. And reconnect the ethereal culture of data, algorithms, and bytes to the thick, dirty materiality of the mineral components that compose it—wires and dust. There is no such thing as clean technology because it is all embedded and grounded in specific material location, labor relations, and geopolitical forces. ——— The crucial ideas I want to emphasize are material locations and perspectivism. The latter is a notion that Spinoza and Leibnitz explored in continental philosophy, which Gilles Deleuze rediscovered and redesigned last century (Deleuze, 1988; 1990; 1993). New materialist philosophies foreground the notion of immanence and the self-organizing vitality of matter, including bodies of all species, sexes, and compositions (Deleuze, 2003). They stress the idea that all living entities are variations on common material forces and elementary particles. Moreover, in a twist that I take as constitutive of the posthuman predicament, they extend the vitality of matter to the technological apparatus, given that contemporary technology is capable of going "live," producing "smart" things and self-correcting artificial intelligence networks, objects, and relations. ——— This dynamic—or vital—vision of materialism extends beyond the classical oppositions of matter/mind and nature/culture, while it also avoids essentialistic holism. The contemporary emphasis on the self-organizing capacity of matter therefore does not assume a sacred natural whole, structured by hierarchical differences of sex, gender, race, class, and species. Posthuman new materialism rather proposes a grounded differential system that works by processes of internal differentiation. Differences function as modulations within a common matter. This view consequently rejects flat equivalences across all species, entities, organisms, and apparatus. It recognizes instead the importance of differences, but rather in the nondualistic and nonhierarchical form of relational bonds, and trans-sex/gender, interclass, cross-generations, multispecies interconnections (Braidotti, 2022). ——— But perspectives and locations were also developed by feminist, critical race, and postcolonial thinkers today, and by much older Indigenous philosophies (Rose, 2004; Viveiros de Castro, 2015; Todd, 2015; Kuokkanen, 2017). On a methodological level, therefore, to assess this posthuman convergence, you need to draw your own cartography in order to visualize your point of entry. How one navigates the posthuman convergence ethically, affectively, and epistemically is a matter of debate and divergence. People can go into complete euphoria about the great perspective of the posthuman horizon, in particular the "Silicon Valley" type of people (Kurzweil, 2006). And others may sink into profound, posthuman melancholia, thinking that there is no future and that it is all over. Cartographies are affective exercises as well as conceptual ones—diverse and heterogeneous, they function like weather maps. ——— People such as yourself, who are working in design, are almost ideally positioned. You can take your bearing from the Earth—the social, urban structures—and your own critical awareness, thereby combining the environmental, the social, and the psychic dimensions. These are some of the ecologies that frame the cartographic effort of accounting for the posthuman convergence. And you even have a market to deal with, so you are not short of coordinates to define your point of entry, both at the level of discourse and of practice.

THE INCIDENTS

The Anthropo-meme

The condition we are in is also known as the crisis of the
Anthropocene, when the specter of extinction raises its ugly
head and haunts the prosperous parts of the world, as well as
those more accustomed to hardship. The Anthropocene is
supposed to be the geological time during which humanity's
negative effect upon the planet's health and sustainability has
reached empirically measurable levels (Crutzer and Stoermer,
2000). The impact is multilayered and it mobilizes our multiple
ecologies of belonging, triggering unprecedented problems
of an environmental, social-economical, and as-affective psychi-
cal character. ——— My position is that the posthuman
condition includes, but also exceeds, the specific framework
of the Anthropocene, which is a popular, albeit controversial,
notion in the scientific community. I am unhappy with this
one-sided rendition of the complex times we are going through.
I long for more precision and higher complexity. The crisis
of the Anthropocene is in fact compounded by the combina-
tion of fast technological advances on the one hand and the
exacerbation of economic and social inequalities on the other,
making for a multifaceted and conflict-ridden landscape in the
context of climate change. In some way, simply referring to the
Anthropocene therefore begs the question. ——— Separating
the different branches of the posthuman convergence is not
helpful, however, because it causes a sort of segregation of
critical insights. In contemporary scholarship, work on AI,
on the Anthropocene, on the new political economy of post-
work, and on climate change and extinction are producing
their respective takes on the human/non-human independently
of one another. ——— I would like to suggest, therefore, two
interrelated moves: that we avoid separating out the different

facets of the convergence and that we look more critically at the notion of the Anthropocene. ——— First of all, the term has not reached scientific consensus. You researchers will all be safer using "climate change science" as a point of reference instead. Essentially, the International Geological Society has not been convinced by the argument. There are not enough traces of negative human impact on the geological structure and strata of our planet to justify the change of our geological era to something called the Anthropocene. ——— Secondly, the term Anthropocene itself has entered a spin. Even as a relative neologism, the Anthropocene has already become another "anthropomeme" (Macfarlane, 2016), spawning several alternative terms, such as "Chthulucene" (Haraway, 2016), "Capitalocene" (Moore, 2013), "Anthropo-scene" (Lorimer, 2017), "Anthrobscene" (Parikka, 2015a), "Plasti-cene" (New York Times, 2014), "Plantationcene" (Tsing, 2015), and "Mis-anthropocene" (Clover and Spahr, 2014). ——— The terminological vitality here reflects a speedy and self-replicating discursive economy. It also expresses both the excite-ment and the exasperation involved in attempting to account for the posthuman predicament. ——— Entering a spin is a form of nomadism or epistemic accelerationism that I ana-lyze with the philosophy of Deleuze and Guattari in terms of territorializations and deterritorializations (Braidotti, 2018). That is to say, an idea—any really good idea—is put out there and it starts circulating, gathering momentum and undergoing multiple mutations along the way. I am especially interested in the different speed of these spins and what their impact is on the multiple levels of our ecologies—environmental, social, and psycho-affective. In other words, I want to track the multiple patterns of subjectivation they engender. ——— Speed and complexity are central to the discursive political economy and the epistemological energy of cognitive capitalism. Given the fluidity of the system, therefore, it is crucial—methodologically as well as strategically—to hold a frame of analysis long enough to take a cartographic shot of the situation. I see this as the main function of posthuman critical theory. The impact of the convergence effect is that it forces us to hold internally contradictory ideas in a precarious but necessary balance. I believe that we need to look at the posthuman as something that is not only an ending, and not only a transition, but also an incredible period of growth and a breathtaking scientific revolution with far-reaching consequences. How to find adequate representation of such complexity is the challenge. ——— To match this complexity, I therefore propose to widen the picture and take a broader look at the posthuman predicament by focusing on the issue of subjectivity. What kind of subjects are we becoming in this context? Because "we" differ in our materially embedded positions of power/access/entitlements; as I argued above, "we" experience the Anthropocene in dramatically different ways. Wealth, class, race, ethnicity, gender and sex, good health, and physical abilities are all intersectional factors that affect our relationship to the specter of extinction—of humans as well as nonhumans. ——— If you look at the Anthropocene scholarship, you will find it obsessed with extinction: learning to die in the Anthropocene is the *leitmotif* (Scranton, 2015). There is a great deal of scholarship of the lament circulating of the proximity of something that looks like human extinction. To some, this apocalyptic vision looks like a massive attack of white, middle-aged anthropocentric panic; to others, extinction is a planetary issue affecting all the inhabitants of the planet: fish, bees, animals, plants. Many blame the excess of capitalist consumption (plastic money, plastic shopping bags) as the main cause. For others, however, the posthuman in a pretext for the enhancement of human capacities and technologically mediated progress that involves space travel, generative medicine, and cryonic dreams of immortality. One way or the other, this conjuncture forces us to address what binds us together—to what an extent we can say to be in this predicament together.

It is undeniable, however, that swinging moods and conflicting affects are a key element of the posthuman mindset. In the posthuman condition, we alternate between moments of euphoria at the thought of the astonishing technological advances "we" are accomplishing, to periods of anxiety in view of the exceedingly high price "we"—both human and nonhumans—are paying for these transformations (Braidotti, 2002). ——— As inhabitants of this planet, alongside many nonhuman inhabitants, we are fatally attracted to the imaginary of disaster. And the interminable wave of disaster movies that the Hollywood dream-and-nightmare machine continues to produce shows that fear of extinction is very profitable. There's money in the imaginary of catastrophe. The plot of these movies follows a predictable format, almost a template: white man lost his woman and is lonely and forlorn, often with his dog, a rifle, and the iconic pickup truck. In the meantime, the planet is dying all around. Alien invasions abound. And it's always about a white man, often older, looking for the one surviving, suitable white girl left on the planet. Think of the second *Blade Runner* film—what a tragedy! This oedipalized plot, with heavy doses of white anguish and male self-pity, codes the social imaginary of disaster movies. The fatal attraction of images of self-destruction prevents us from looking further to all the other elements of the contemporary social and affective landscape, framed by the posthuman convergence. ——— I prefer, therefore, to draw your attention to the serious scholarship of anxiety currently produced. There is so much of it that I coedited the *Posthuman Glossary* (2018) and *More Posthuman Glossary* (2022) to provide a selective overview. To name a few: Francis Fukuyama's *Our Posthuman Future* (2002)—the leader of neoliberal laissez-faire politics, who didn't want to regulate anything, now wants to regulate human nature. What he has in mind is to preserve and possibly increase the demographics of whites and Caucasians, in the framework of the transhumanists' takeover of human evolution. Jürgen Habermas, after he converted to Catholicism and published his conversation with Cardinal Ratzinger, published *The Future of Human Nature* (2003). He expresses concern bordering on moral panic about the future of humanistic values and human dignity, threatened by advanced technologies. Peter Sloterdijk (2009), rewriting Heidegger's *Letter on Humanism* about the human zoo, shares this anxiety about the status of the *human* in our advanced technological times. ——— And then His Holiness Pope Francis, whom I find very *sympatique*, entered the debate. I especially value his Encyclical Letter *Laudato Si* (2015) on caring for the earth, our common home. Pope Francis is very much a climate change activist, and he actually veers toward the Capitalocene, because he blames capitalism for the current disaster. When he organized his seminar at Castel Gandolfo on climate change, the Pope chose his own keynote speaker in addition to all the cardinals and the traditionalists. And you may know who Pope Francis invited: Naomi Klein, to speak about her analysis of the destructive role of capitalism.[1] It is worth looking at the faces of the cardinals while she speaks. ——— Incidentally, a useful teaching exercise is to select a couple of pages of that Encyclical letter, take off the name of the author, and then ask students to guess who wrote it. Often a sizable proportion of my class guesses Felix Guattari. And it is a close guess, within the tradition of continental naturalism (Pearson and Protevi, 2016). But of course, in the case of Pope Francis, his thought is structured by the whole fabric of natural law and moral phi-losophy. In the case of Guattari (1995) on the other hand, you will find materialist vitalism with Spinoza, heterogeneity, and complex assemblages. These are two very different approaches, but they both embrace matter as alive and self-organizing, so they are closer than they seem. ——— Be that as it may, the affective and emotional economy is crucial in the posthuman convergence: the swinging moods, the anxiety, the fear, the melancholia, and, let's face it, the general depression. And if it is true that we are approaching the point of irreversibility in climate change, those negative passions are understandable. If the end is near, why bother? And this deep disaffection hangs heavily over the future generations, stirring deep emotions and leaving so many questions unanswered. This is one of the reasons I have focused on affirmative ethics, to which I will return. ——— For now, let me stress the importance of using critique also for clinical purposes, to lift our spirits a bit and make complex things thinkable, instead of letting them be so opaque and oppressive. Instead of giving in to the self-indulgent imaginary of disaster, I would like to propose that we pursue this discussion about loss and death through a serious critique of the posthuman convergence, including the necro-political character of cognitive capitalism.

1. For The Guardian's coverage of Pope Francis's invitation, see Rosie Scammell, "Pope Francis recruits Naomi Klein in climate change battle," *The Guardian*, June 27, 2015, https://www.theguardian.com/world/2015/jun/28/pope-climate-change-naomi-klein.

Cognitive Capitalism

What constitutes capital value today, in addition to the more traditional forms of labor exploitation, is the informational power of living matter—its immanent qualities and self-organizing capacity. Our universities are in the middle of these phenomenal and exciting developments—we are motors of what has become known as "cognitive capitalism" (Moulier-Boutang, 2012). Examples are synthetic biology, stem cell research, nanotechnologies, robotics, neural sciences, and information technologies. The biogenetic structure of contemporary capitalism enhances the ability to generate profits from the scientific and economic comprehension of all that lives. ———— This includes many classes of disposable humans: underpaid, often unregistered migrant workers who provide the manual labor in agriculture, building, transportation, and assembling work, constituting the digital proletariat of today. This new political economy is also called: "the politics of Life itself" (Rose, 2001), also known as "Life as surplus" (Cooper, 2008), or, quite simply as the postgenomic economy of "bio-capital" (Rajan, 2006). The true capital today is the vital, self-organizing power of converging technologies whose vitality seems unsurpassable and exceeds the speed of the human brain and neural system. ———— The consumption of commodities and the sell-ability of the informational data mined from all organisms are central to contemporary capitalism and contribute to its continuing disregard for the environment. The classical Vitruvian Man is completely commodified into a system where planned obsolescence, and design that kills time, is also an integral part of how we live and what we do. Cognitive capitalism capitalizes at top speed on all that lives. Codes—biogenetic codes, algorithmic codes—allow for endless quantification and data collection, and capitalizing on them is the real thing. Farming, saving, and selling every bit of information they can mine are the true capital. ——— The social consequences are problematic. Let me refer to Thomas Piketty's study of the economic disparities of our times, with the great tech firms that run our universe. We are in a period of capitalism where the concentration of wealth is higher than it was when Charles Dickens denounced the first industrial revolution. The contrast between the extent of the poverty and the cumulation of wealth is simply abhorrent, with the 12 richest people on earth owning as much as half of the rest of the world's population. ——— To say that these social inequalities create enormous problems would be an understatement. And it is not surprising that so many are tempted by a return to Marxism-Leninism, although this ideology didn't produce great results during the previous century. It may be more relevant right now to take stock instead of the contradictions of the Fourth Industrial Revolution and the Sixth Extinction. Let's try to be *unsentimental* and a little bit lucid about the posthuman convergence. Partly because, as people of science and as scholars, we really owe it to our intelligence to also rejoice in what we, as an academic community, have produced as a most extraordinary scientific and technological apparatus. Cognitive capitalism is a research-driven system that profits from the knowledge and power over all that lives. ——— Let me take the example of synthetic biology, more specifically of artificial meat grown on a petri dish from a small amount of stem cells. The first synthetic hamburger made in the Netherlands in 2013 cost $325,000. A few years later, the prices dropped to $11 per synthetic hamburger. We environmentalists, vegans, and animal rights and transnational environmental justice activists should be dancing with joy at the news. Synthetic meat could completely reorganize our agricultural-industrial complex, the cattle industry, and the biotechnology of food production. The environmental consequences would be huge and to the benefit of the planet; it would be life-changing. Of course, it would cost thousands, even millions of jobs, and this would require careful planning and conversion. And yet every time I mention artificial meat, there is a slight sense of discomfort in the audience, who often looks utterly disgusted. A synthetic hamburger may have all the right proteins and nutritional properties, but it is still most unappetizing and slightly off-putting. ——— If we stay with that troublesome reaction for a bit, let me ask: What do you miss when meat becomes de-linked from the animal body and is thus dematerialized? When we emancipate the meat from its organic roots? That feeling of loss and dispossession is also called *eco-nostalgia*, and I think it's a far more widespread sentiment than we give it credit for. I find it significant on several scores. Firstly, because it shows the importance of our being embodied and embedded, and how attached we are not only to our bodily roots, but also those of other species. ——— This reaction of eco-nostalgia and technophobia, or fear of biotech, also shows to what an extent anthropomorphism is constitutive of us humans and how deeply it affects our own sense of belonging to this particular species and our relationship to the world. Feeling disgusted by artificial meat, however, exposes at the same time our uncritical reliance on eating other species. It therefore brings forth our deeply seated anthropocentrism, the reliance on naturalized others—such as animals—as objects of consumption, while we humans actually remain unaware of our sense of entitlement. It is one thing to be anthropomorphic, embodied and embedded as members of our species, but quite another to be anthropocentric and settle in our self-referential system. ——— The example of synthetic meat reveals the defining features of cognitive capitalism, which I read with Deleuze and Guattari, *A Thousand Plateaus: Capitalism and Schizophrenia* (1977; 1987). This is a post-binary, that is to say rhizomatic, system, in constant flows of de-/re-territorializations. Knowledge-producing and research-driven, it is a nonlinear and multidirectional, and it flows without any teleological aim. Furthermore, it produces another significant paradox: as a result of mining the basic codes and informational data of multiple organisms as well as ourselves, the categorical distinction between the human and other species is blurred, if not actually erased, when it comes to profiting from them. ——— Seeds, cells, plants, animals, and bacteria, but also codes, algorithms, and networks fit into this logic of commodification, alongside various specimens of humanity, producing an opportunistic form of post-anthropocentrism that spuriously unifies all the species under the imperative of profit. The excesses of the "Capitalocene" threaten the uniqueness of Anthropos, as well as the sustainability of the planet as a whole. ——— A vital new materialist philosophy, based on rereading the Spinozist ontology and applying it to our understanding of capitalism, is both in dialogue but also disagreement with the Marxist-Leninist analysis of capital. The philosophical discussion here is between Spinoza and Hegel, to paraphrase an important study by Pierre Macherey, which was written in 1979 and was translated into English only in 2011, back-to-back with the explosion of interest in Deleuze. That study helps us understand the importance of the move accomplished by advanced capitalism toward cognitive control over living matter. ——— Cognitive capitalism is an axiomatic system that capitalizes on living matter—natural, cultural, technological—making money out of everything without any concern for the future. It is a system that undermines its own conditions that, if it is a "future eater" (Flannery, 1994), erodes its own foundations and sabotages the conditions of possibility for its own survival. Vandana Shiva (1997) quite rightly calls it *bio-piracy*—the perpetual theft of the living properties of matter. To understand a system that functions like this, we need to learn to think differently about the work of critique. We have to evolve from dialectical habits of thought based on dualistic oppositions to a grounded, new materialist critique based on a nature-culture continuum, which means that differences are variations within a common matter. If we are all part of a system that capitalizes on all that lives, "we"—remember, positioned differently within different perspectives—need to work from within, from our respective locations, to make interventions that can make a difference. (Braidotti, 2022) ——— The contemporary posthuman moment displays also inhumane aspects and a large share of cruelty to account for. The brutality of new power relations has established a necro-political mode of governing, which targets not only the management of the living, but also multiple practices of managed decline and planned dying (Foucault, 1977; 1978). ——— Consider, for example, the generalized material destruction of human bodies, populations, and the environment through the industrial-scale warfare led by drones and other unmanned vehicles. Think also of the global effects of migration as a result of dispossession, wards, expulsions, climate change, and terror. The refugee camps and other zones of detention are multiplying, as are our militarized borders and humanitarian interventions. Whole sections of humanity are downgraded to the status of infra-humans, extraterritorial, like refugees and the asylum seekers, whom we treat as alien others, not meant to be here at all. ——— Let it be clear, therefore, that, far from marking the extinction or the impoverishment of the human, the posthuman condition is a way of reconstituting the human—for some even as a return to neo-humanist values, coupled with forms of enhancement. There are many dynamics of subject formation coming into being in this posthuman conjunction as a result of the dislocation of the ontological grounds on which the human used to be composed and experienced socially.

Many of these concerns reverberate across the knowledge currently produced. Posthuman scholarship constitutes a transdisciplinary field that is more than the sum of its parts and points to a qualitative leap toward the construction of different fields of knowledge: the Critical Posthumanities. The creativity and exuberance of the field, the scale and the quantity of the work being done in the posthuman convergence, is such that it is nonsense to speak of humanities in crisis. There is rather huge growth, coupled with a shift of paradigm. ——— The posthuman convergence is a way of framing this oscillating "yes, but" element, that is to say of interrogating where critical thinking is going in an era where critical theory is not held in high esteem, and the STEMs and life sciences are so central to the academic world. So, the posthuman is an indicator of our historicity, and it is also a navigational tool. It leads to questions such as: What kind of subjects are we becoming? What is happening to us? And there are many dynamics of subject formation coming into being in such posthuman conjunction. Deleuze would say it is a conceptual persona that helps us illuminate what's happening to us. ——— I turn to the scholarship for answers and study which discourses are ongoing about our common humanity. There are already multiple forms of posthumanism: insurgent (Papadopoulos, 2010), speculative (Sterling, 2012; Roden, 2014), cultural (Herbrechter, 2013), literary (Nayar, 2013), transhumanism (Bostrom, 2014), metahumanism (Ferrando, 2013), a-humanism (MacCormack, 2014), posthuman manifesto (Pepperell, 2003), and a post-humanities book series (Wolfe, 2011). And the differences between them, which I also outlined in the two glossaries I coedited, are less relevant than the commonalities. These are all discourses that come out from faculties that still call themselves the humanities. ——— Let me focus on the most dominant of these discourses, which I consider as the ethos of cognitive capitalism, namely transhumanism. Institutionally based in Oxford, in an institute called no less than the Institute for the Future of Humanity and directed by Nick Bostrom, the transhumanists have elaborated and formalized the axiom of cognitive capitalism. And the axiom is as follows: analytically, we are posthumanists, we know that we have a Fourth Industrial Revolution and a Sixth Extinction. We have AI. And we have a problem with climate change. We have synthetic biology, and we have drought and bushfire. Normatively, however, our values are neo-humanist. This internally contradictory balancing act between analytic post-anthropocentrism and normative neo-humanism allows Bostrom to have his posthuman cake and eat it too. In other words, he presents posthuman evolution through technological enhancement as the accomplishment of the Enlightenment, defined as a rationalist project based on channeling and perfecting the abilities of humanity through science and technology. ——— The transhumanist argument is that nowadays humanity is failing under the weight of the incredibly intelligent computational systems that we have created ourselves. Our brain is much slower than the computational systems we have designed. A lot of scholars in media studies are on to it, as are neural and cognitive scientists. So, what are we going to do? We are going to enhance the human and accelerate our neural responses. Human enhancement. That is the core of the Oxford transhumanists. The project is called Superintelligence, and it is extremely well-funded. Although Cambridge has set up a Centre for the Study of Existential Risk, human enhancement remains an experimental project. And as a feminist and anti-racist, I worry about selection criteria and implementation policies: who gets chosen for what kind of enhancement and who does not even qualify for the first selection. ———— Transhumanism speaks both to capital's desire to control the levers of evolution and to the humanists' aspiration to perfection. But it does not entail any sustained critical effort to be inclusive and democratic about its experiments with what the human is capable of becoming. My critical posthuman stance is a way of calling this dominant technological and financial movement to accountability. ———— There are of course other institutional models, and in Europe the situation is a little more diversified. I am thinking of the Posthumanities Hub at the University of Linkoping in Sweden, which does bring in both the critique of humanism and the critique of anthropocentrism. They include the feminist angle, critical race theory, decolonial thought, and migration, all while looking seriously at the environment—a perfect example of posthuman theory at work (Asberg and Braidotti, 2018). ———— A broader experiment relying on the arts and media activism as research method has been conducted in Germany by the Haus der Kulturen der Welt in Berlin. It enlists design and media in trying to come to terms with the big posthuman convergence. Although the first academic journal devoted to posthuman studies has a solid academic basis,[2] the field is much broader and it includes a sizable corporate, as well as arts and design, sector. It is interesting to note the role of design, media, museums, and nonacademic institutions in posthuman scholarship: these nonacademic venues have a significant impact on knowledge production practices. ———— It is indeed one of the features of cognitive capitalism that knowledge production is no longer the monopoly or the prerogative of institutions like the university, which for centuries has been the privileged site of knowledge, science, and truth. Knowledge production is now a process distributed across society, to become coextensive with the social field as a whole. There's so much knowledge being produced outside academic institutions that the universities sometimes struggle to keep up. And with the accelerations of the posthuman condition, the gap is almost painful. The good side of it is that the academic institutions now acknowledge that we need the creators, the designers, the artists, the engineers—that is to say the forces of the imagination—as well as the rigor of academic methods. The question of what the university itself can do and how the academic disciplines will interact with the posthuman challenges, however, remains open.

2. See Stefan Lorenz Sorgner (editor in chief) and Sangkyu Shin (ex officio editor), *Journal of Posthuman Studies: Philosophy, Technology, Media* (University Park: The Pennsylvania State University Press).

The Critical Posthumanities

What are we to make of this proliferation of discourses and institutional practices? I want to demonstrate the vitality of posthuman scholarship and argue that qualitative innovations are being produced collectively, and in transdisciplinary ways. My argument is that the posthuman convergence is registered within the academic world through the explosion of fields that I call the Critical Posthumanities. They are new areas of study that seldom coincide with the traditional humanities and are concentrated in a number of creative transdisciplinary hubs, which have generated their own hybrid offsprings. They call themselves ecological, environmental, sustainable, interactive, digital, medical, public humanities. ———— What I first want to comment on is that they actually call themselves the humanities. But what are their building blocks? Over the last thirty years, major theoretical innovation in the humanities has emerged from a number of often radical and always interdisciplinary discourses that called themselves "studies." You can look at what I call the first generation of critical studies: women's, gender, feminist, queer, race, postcolonial, subaltern, cultural, film, theater, television and media, and performance studies, but also science and technology studies in a number of different versions. ———— These "studies" share a number of features: they voice the situated knowledges of the dialectical and structural "others" of humanistic "Man"; they criticize the idea of the human implicitly upheld by the academic humanities on two grounds: structural anthropocentrism on the one hand and in-built Eurocentrism and "methodological nationalism" (Beck, 2007) on the other. ———— They also expose the compatibility of rationality and violence, of scientific progress on the one hand and practices of structural exclusion on the other. Institutionally, they are in constant critical negotiations with the rules, conventions, and protocols of the academic disciplines. This nomadic exodus from disciplinary "homes" shifts the point of reference away from the authority of the past and onto accountability for the present. ——— They are both critical—of dominant visions of knowing subjects—and creative—by actualizing the virtual and unrealized insights and competences of marginalized subjects (Braidotti, 2002; 2006). And they do so in a manner that makes the lives of the excluded not only visible, but also productive of knowledge. It is a way of showing the knowledge that is being produced at what we used to call the *margins*. ——— Let me give you an example that is dear to my heart. A significant alliance between queer theorists and the science fiction horror genre has grown into a fast-growing posthuman feminist strand. Since the 1970s, feminist writers and literary theorists of science fiction (Kristeva, 1980; Barr, 1987, 1993; Haraway, 1992; Creed, 1993) had supported the alliance between women, as the others of Man, and such other "others" as the sexualized others (women, LGBTQ+), the racialized others (non-whites, postcolonial, Black, Jewish, Indigenous, and migrant subjects), and the naturalized nonhumans (animals, insects, plants, trees, viruses, and bacteria). I think it is a perfectly reasonable alliance of all those who fall short of standard definitions of the human as Man—the marginalized, the excluded, the downtrodden, the disqualified—women, LGBTQ+, trans, migrants, the animals, the machines; all those who are "othered," united against the empire of white "Man." ——— I would say feminist theory, feminism, race and Indigenous philosophies, together with Afrofuturism and forms of anti-racism, are the theories that pioneer a sense of exiting from *the human*. And what has *the human* ever done for me? And why should I be loyal to a category that has only ever discriminated against me? Why would I be loyal to this standard? ——— At the level of the political economy, what |we have here is this mushrooming, infrastructural effect, which was the evolution of the *studies* discourses that really promoted interdisciplinarity, connection to the real world, radical thinking, and critical theory for decades. Most of these are still here. I see the first generation of critical studies as basically taking on humanism, and taking on the limitations of a certain idea of Man. ——— Three critical remarks: firstly, not all these "studies" simply opposed humanism to embrace the posthuman: they also offered alternative visions of the humanist self, knowledge, and society. Notions such as a female/feminist humanity (Irigaray, 1993), queer humanism, and Black humanity (Fanon, 1967) are part of this tradition of more inclusive humanism (Braidotti and Gilroy, 2016). ——— Secondly, many of these "studies"—but by no means all of them—were activated and propelled by the incisive philosophical, linguistic, cultural, and textual innovations introduced by the French post-structuralist generation since the 1970s. These philosophical frameworks brought alternative perspectives and sources of inspiration to the posthuman moment. ——— Thirdly, the creative proliferation of "studies" is an institutional phenomenon that is unevenly distributed geographically. The conflicting and contradictory receptions of the "studies" during the 1990s "theory wars" in the United States coincided not only with the rise of the political Right, the consequences of which we are all experiencing today, but also with the rise of digital culture, of biogenetic and cognitive capitalism. It also resulted in a profound transformation of the university structure and its integration into neoliberal econom-ics, which included the creation of classes of both academic stars and the academic "precariat." (This neologism merges "precarious" with "proletariat" to designate the bottom social class in advanced capitalism.) ——— The proliferation of "studies" accelerated with the posthuman turn in the Anthropocene, when "Man" came under further criticism as Anthropos, that is to say as a supremacist species that monopolized the right to access the bodies of all living entities. The anthropocentric core of the humanities was also challenged by the ubiquity of technological mediation and the capitalization of Life through data mining, which prompted the opportunistic displacement of the centrality of the human that I commented on before. Decentering anthropo-centric patterns of thought is especially difficult for the humanities, in that it positions terrestrial, planetary, and cosmic concerns, as well as the conventional naturalized others, animals, plants, and the technological apparatus, as serious agents and co-constructors of collective thinking and knowing. ——— What has emerged in the last fifteen years is a second generation of "studies" areas, genealogically indebted to the first generation in terms of critical aims and political effects and commitment to social justice, while addressing more directly the issue of anthropocentrism. For example: Posthuman/inhuman/nonhuman studies, posthuman disability studies, critical animal studies, critical vegan studies, eco-criticism, critical plants studies, post-secular studies, and globalization studies. The exuberant growth and the multiple accelerations just go on. ——— The new materialist turn also plays its hand here: within media theory, for instance, the shift from critiques of representations to the grounded analysis of code itself is significant. Linguistically oriented representational issues are left behind in favor of the material structures of discourse. This neo-materialist approach turns to the study of materials, from geology to meteorology to simple objects—a more design-oriented approach, which is very recent in relation to the traditional concepts and methods of critical theory. ——— A related and equally prolific field of posthuman research concerns the inhuman, and inhumane, aspects of our historical condition: conflict and peace research studies; post-Soviet/communist studies; human rights studies and humanitarian management; migration and mobility studies; trauma, memory, and reconciliation studies; security, death, and suicide studies; extinction studies; and the list is still growing. —— What used to be necropolitical is now breaking down to a number of other areas where the inhumane aspects of the present conditions are in focus. Death studies are a growing area because of the appalling statistics of youth suicide and general burnout. I don't mean this cynically, but with pastoral concern—they are very interesting forms of transdisciplinarity. —— These successive generations of "studies" areas are both institutionally and theoretically the motor of critique and creativity. Dis-identifications from "Man/ Anthropos" occurred in the space of several generations of critical studies along the axes of sexualization: becoming-woman/ LGBTQ+; racialization; becoming-Indigenous/other; naturalization, becoming-earth. —— But the Critical Posthumanities mark a qualitative leap. And it's a very recent one spread over a large range: ecological humanities, environmental humanities, blue humanities, green humanities, sustainable humanities, interactive humanities, organic humanities, greater humanities; medical humanities; bio-humanities; neural-evolutionary humanities; community humanities; public humanities; civic humanities. ——And you will not be surprised to know that the meta-discourses are also following, that there are multiple discourses—the meta-patterning is already happening. The Posthumanities (Wolfe, 2010); the Inhuman Humanities (Grosz, 2011); the Digital Humanities (Hayles, 1990; 2005); Transformative Humanities (Epstein, 2012); Critical Posthumanities (Braidotti, 2013); Nomadic Humanities

(Stimpson, 2016). ——— The methodological question here is: What is happening to posthuman knowledge production, to go from the earlier reliance on critical discourses, discourses that are critical of humanism or critical of anthropocentrism, to a different form, which is coming up with these new humanities of which every major university is richly endowed? I think the Environmental Humanities Initiative at Harvard and Digital Humanities at Duke are pioneers. But by now, every research university has its Environmental Humanities, Digital Humanities —it is like the new mantra. ——— Firstly, let me say that, far from being the symptom of crisis and fragmentation, these new discourses are a sign of great vitality and innovation in the field. There is no crisis of the humanities in terms of content and research energy. The Posthumanities open new eco-sophical, posthumanist, and post-anthropocentric dimensions for the humanities. And—crucial for my materialist carto-graphic method—these developments are empirically verifiable; they are already here. Remember the institutional examples I already showed you. ——— Moreover, it would be superficial to take the ongoing proliferation of new discourses as the mere expression of relativism, let alone the much-despised postmod-ernism. And it may be tempting, but equally lazy, to take the fast growth of the Critical Posthumanities as self-generating. The fact that rhizomic, web-like knowledge production backed by the internet may be going viral does not make it sponta-neous. ——— The Critical Posthumanities are rather the result of the hard work of communities of thinkers, scholars, and activists that reconstitute not only the missing links in aca-demic knowledge practices: it is a collective praxis that assem-bles a missing people. ——— Their defining features are striking: the Critical Posthumanities no longer assume that the subject of knowledge is *homo universalis* or Anthropos.

They're assuming a transversal knowledge-production entity. Transversality, that is to say a more complex, embodied, embedded, non-unitary, relational, and affective transversal subject—my *Nomadic Subjects* (Braidotti, 1994, 2011a; 2011b)—is an example of this. But different scholars are doing complex assemblages with all kinds of other philosophers. You will find a lot of Whitehead and a lot of Wittgenstein, for instance. You will find a massive return of the American pragmatists. A very complex process ontology allows us to think about a transversal subject position. And that transversality is being able to sustain the effort to think the posthuman convergence. In terms of the work ethics, the project is linked to a collaborative morality. And a collaborative morality is the ethics that we get from a contemporary reading of Spinoza's work on joy, which I read as affirmation. ——— So, the posthuman subject is neither universal nor anthropocentric. A collective assemblage, collaboratively linked to a material web of human and nonhuman agents—the subject of knowledge is zoe-/geo-/techno-mediated (Braidotti, 2019). I think you will find the term *assemblage* in a lot of the new materialism discourse—certainly in Katherine Hayles (2016), in DeLanda (2016), and in my own work (Braidotti, 2006; 2013)—as a way of positing a *trans* type of subject that can hold in there, in a process of metastability, in order to cope with the challenges and to try to make sense of what is happening to us, of what we can make of this particular political economy of knowledge production. ——— It also follows that the objects of research and inquiry of the humanities have ceased to be focused exclusively on "Man" and his anthropomorphic others. Today, on top of human diversity, we will find animal studies, eco-, and geo-criticism. In terms of object of study, today the humanities are covering forests, fungi, bacteria, dust, and bio-hydro-solar-techno powers. We have meta-objects and the hyper-sea, "human/imal" and algorithmic cultural studies. ——— It is not just a matter of adopting new objects of inquiry, however, something else has changed, both at the conceptual level and in the methodology. The Critical Posthumanities take on the vital materialism, the life-making capacities of organic entities, but also of inorganic devices. They teach us how to think the vitalist immanence of non-anthropomorphic life systems. Posthuman scholarship celebrates the diversity of zoe— nonhuman life—in a nonhierarchical manner, recognizing the respective degrees of intelligence, ability, and creativity of all organisms. It is not as a "flat ontology," but as a materially embedded differential system within a common matter. This implies that thinking and knowing are not the prerogative of humans alone, but take place in the world, which is the terrestrial, grounded location for multiple thinking species and computational networks—we are all eco-sophically connected.

The Missing People

In terms of attempting a critique, one thing is obvious and clear: that old and new patterns of exclusion are still at work and that the "missing people" are still missing. The usual suspects are not actually being capitalized upon. By "missing people," I appeal to a we-are-in-this-together-but-we-are-not-one-and-the-same kind of posthuman subject—not a new synthesis, but a heterogeneous assemblage. ——— The constitutive "others" are not being territorialized to the same extent. I haven't seen non-nationally-indexed humanities in the literature. Black humanities, migrant/diasporic humanities—I have not seen much institutionalization of these. Poor/trailer-park humanities—I owe this to Richard Rorty in his 1998 master-piece *Achieving Our Country*, where he talks about the dispos-sessed poor whites, predicting they will radicalize to the Right. But the decolonial humanities are missing too, as are the child's humanities, and the otherwise-abled or disabled human-ities. They are present in the scholarship, but not the institutional reality. So, do we have an emergent situation here where the people that have been the usual suspects of exclusions and marginalization are once again being left out of the posthuman picture? Or are there signs that there is actually a convergence between the socially excluded and the new discourses of the humanities? ——— Historically, all sorts of communities were already empirically missing. Whether we look at women and LGBTQ+, Indigenous knowledge systems, at queers, otherwise enabled, trailer parks, nonhumans, or technologically mediated existences, these are real-life subjects whose knowledge never made it into any of the official cartographies. Their struggle for visibility and emergence also affects the knowledge they are capable of generating. ——— But the other missing people are the virtual ones, those that can emerge only as the result of a neo-materialist praxis of affirmation, aimed at constructing the plane of composition for such an assembly. This composition requires affirmative relational alliances of a high degree of subtlety and complexity. They need to go beyond identity claims, not by denying them, but by expanding them into diversified embedded and embodied materialist platforms of different "missing people."

———— There is strong evidence now of planetary, differential Posthumanities, as I call them. Indigenous environmental and digital humanities, for instance, is quite a movement, often led by graduate students, budding and emerging, but very strong online. Many websites and networks are being designed, where the Indigenous perspective and land rights perspective meet the Anthropocene, meet the legal issues, meet the representational issues, meet the cognitive issues, producing a different way of doing the Posthumanities. *Postcolonial Green* is pretty well established in comparative literature. Queer neo-humanism is seen in a variety of ways, but is very much at the center of the discussion because of the perspectivist approach. ———— These assemblages of the issues of land rights, Indigenous philosophies, and posthuman thought are a debated and fraught area, not at all a harmonious synthesis. I see them as zones of encounter and hence of contestation, and thus incredibly alive. Let us not forget that for so many populations under the sun—populations that have been depleted by colonial violence—extinction is a sad reality, and they are the engineers of survival as well as the oldest shepherds of the earth. So, the discussion of what used to be postcolonial theory is being reshaped in a very material manner through the encounter with Indigenous epistemologies in the posthuman convergence. ———— Different assemblages are being formed along the convergence of posthumanism and post-anthropocentrism, but adding in the social, ethical, and political dimensions. They follow an encounter between feminist, LGBTQ+, and gender studies; postcolonial, de-colonial, and indigenous studies; critical legal studies; media activists; hackers and makers; and First National land rights activists.

———— These encounters are transforming both the critical environmental and digital posthumanities. The assemblages they compose are as multiple as their lived experience, producing new areas of research, such as the transnational, justice, postcolonial, environmental, and digital humanities.

THE INCIDENTS

To sustain the effort, "we" need a new collective subject, a "we"-are-in-this-together kind of subject, but not as One and the Same. This can be understood as a process of becoming in its own immanence and not in binary oppositional terms. This is a we-are-in-this-together kind of people that are anxious and in turmoil because of the times, internally fractured and not at all the same or universal, determined to adopt a critical and creative stance toward the great opportunities, but also the injustices and threats of present times. ——— The materially embedded differential "we" is actualized in a process of becoming other-than-the Homo Universalis of humanism or other-than-the Anthropos of anthropocentrism. The politics of immanence compose planes of becoming for a missing people that was never fully part of the "human," whose crisis so preoccupies the "humanities" today. ——— Posthuman subjectivity can be supported by a subtler and more diversified affective range that avoids the polarization between mourning (apocalyptic variant) and celebration (euphoric variable) in relation to humanity as both a vulnerable and an insurgent category. ——— *Affirmative ethics* is what I have proposed. It is a collective praxis of co-construction of sustainable alternatives designed for the challenges of the posthuman convergence. It is the hard work of extracting knowledge from the pain of exclusion and turning it into workable solutions for the world we are living in. Together. ——— For me, then, the issue more than ever is, how can *we*, as people who are committed to think our way through this posthuman convergence; how can *we*, who are in this together but are not one and the same; how can *we* develop a set of values, of attributes, of terminologies whereby we can think differently but together about the challenges, the contradictions, the exhilaration, and the exhaustion of the Fourth Industrial Revolution and the Sixth Extinction together in a materially embedded way, becoming in and with the world? Because guys, we only have one of those. Thank you.

AUDIENCE: [*Applause*]

JOHN: We have some time for questions. I'm going to start with one. Rosi, I'm just curious. One of the issues, I think, that has arisen at the GSD, and I'm sure in many other institutions, is what to do with the canon. That's not really a new question in a lot of ways, but I wonder if you could just give a few of your thoughts because you're quite open in your own work about the debt that your work pays to philosophical traditions that, in certain ways, may have been exclusionary or carry many of the exclusionary aspects that you've described tonight. ——— How do you take on this double-edged sword of the canon in your own teaching? We're dealing with it here at the GSD, not only in terms of the textual canon, but also the architectural canon and how we might restructure certain kinds of courses, to simultaneously open those up, but at the same time retain what was good and what can be retained of the tradition of humanism.

ROSI: You're asking one of the easy questions, aren't you? Thank you very much. I have, of course, like many people of my generation, a double sort of disciplinary origin. I am very much part of the continental philosophical tradition, and very much part of radical feminism, radical anti-fascism, radical anti-racism. Multiple genealogies. I would say that is true of most critical thinkers. Of course, you rely on a canon. You grow up in a canon. You indulge in a canon. But you are fed by multiple other sources. ———— I think that diversity of sources is crucial because I would not want any disciplinary purity. In a sense, I don't even believe that there is such a thing as a canon, but there are disciplinary ecologies of *belonging*. I'm warning if anybody is in philosophy out there, however, that as one grows older, one's original discipline beckons back. And texts that you used to read at 20 come back to haunt you. And you think, I can't believe I'm rereading this one again. So, a discipline is an incredible passion, and philosophy is one hell of a discipline. But so are the radical epistemologies that led to the critical work on this. How I do this is, again, by being merrily nomadic and respectfully disloyal to my disciplines. After all, I am rooted but I flow. ———— As a feminist philosopher, I have a lifelong disagreement with the masculinism and Eurocentrism of my discipline. But it is often easier to critique and even dismiss the disciplinary rules and boundaries, because of their denial of sexual difference, gender blindness, and the worship of the dead white males. Far more difficult to develop an affirmative response and come up with alternatives. As a careful reader of Spinoza and Deleuze, as well as the feminist tradition, I am aware that I am myself very much part of the problem of the canon, in so far as I am involved in preserving the legacy of those philosophers. ———— So, to make amends, I embarked on one of the most demanding intellectual projects of my life: I coedited a volume of a massive history of continental philosophy. Under the general editorship of Alan Schrift, the eight-volume project took years to complete. I was in charge of volume seven, which covers 1980 to 1995, the fallout of post-structuralism (Braidotti, 2010). I did it precisely as a way of settling the score with my beloved discipline, and it was a confronting but rewarding experience. In addition to the general introduction and the feminist philosophy chapter, I also cowrote the conclusion of that volume with my friend Judith Butler. We adopted a personal tone in that chapter and commented on the complex relationship we both had to our discipline, the institutional frictions we experienced in our career, and our painful separation from it. Even or especially for radical thinkers, the issue of how to relate to the history of a patriarchal discipline such as philosophy is never resolved. ——— My posthumanist stance did not ease matters in philosophical circles. If you are in the neurosciences, you can refer to Damasio; if you are in genetics, to McClintock; in evolutionary biology, to Margulis in order to demonstrate the simple case that we are all part of the same matter. But to make the same assertion in the humanities and say we are in a continuum with nature is a scandal. One gets suspected of biological determinism, particularly with the history of vital materialism being complicitous with the hierarchical politics of fascism and colonialism. The nature-culture divide is crucial for the humanities, and you challenge it at your own risk and peril. In other words, even in the humanities, the dominant, hegemonic methodology is social constructivism—one is not born, one becomes—and that dualistic approach, perfected in the twentieth century does not allow us to think a nature-culture continuum. ——— The post-structuralist philosophical generation addressed directly the question of the canon, especially Deleuze who in some ways rewrote the institutional curriculum and brought to the fore the more marginal, half-forgotten traditions. He argues that within the continental tradition, there are counter histories of philosophy, that is to say texts that teach us to think differently. Spinoza, for instance, allows us to think a nature-culture continuum. And incidentally that's why Hegel was so irritated with Spinoza, just like today's Marxists, Badiou and Žižek, for instance, are so irritated with neo-Spinozists like Deleuze.

———— Leaving aside this polemic, I think it's safer for younger researchers to go back to the past and, say, dig out lesser-known figures within the canon and show that we do have these alternatives in our tradition. The Stoics come to mind. Stoicism is focused on learning to die, especially in Marcus Aurelius, Montaigne, and Seneca—all of them are incredibly relevant to the debates about the posthuman convergence. These are thinkers who prepare us to die. ———— Instead of getting into a fit of Anthropocene-driven anxiety, you are better off reading some Seneca, doing some Stoicism. And then maybe we can pursue this conversation. ———— Thinking about time is crucial, and I have argued that the present is not one block of either anxiety or of excitement. It's not one thing. It's *a thousand plateaus* of temporal complexities. In fact, the formula that I offer in the present is both the record of what we are ceasing to be and the seed of what we are in the process of becoming, simultaneously. The actual and the virtual. ———— So, you can engage with the present like the record of what we are ceasing to be. And we are ceasing to be defined in relation to Man. We are also ceasing to be Anthropos. But we are also in the process of becoming a thousand other things. And this is exactly what is at stake in the posthuman convergence: the transformations and mutations of the human. Considering the hegemony of the transhumanist paradigm, some of the options worry me a bit, especially the fate of the "missing people." ———— The crucial thing however is to get activated to think through these challenges and not to cave in, believing that this is the unthinkable. And why would a convergence, however multiscalar and complex, be unthinkable? And what is the regime of thinkability that we are applying to the analysis of the posthuman predicament? And part of my contribution is to try to make this condition very thinkable, and to develop an affirmative mode of relation to it. ———— I am also very cautious about methods and strategies in relation to the canon, on behalf of the starting researchers. My advice to you is not to fall out of the canon. We want you to go on, get your PhD, become professors, run the world. Don't drop out. Drop in. Do the work and revive within the tradition other sources, in a dialogue with multiple other references that come from other cultures and other traditions. It is hard work, but I firmly believe that *we* can do it.

AUDIENCE: My name is Jannis, from East Asian Studies and Civilizations. So as an area studies scholar, my question is if posthumanism can truly offer a point of entry for scholars like ours who are in area studies, as in all the studies that you present show that area studies is missing. So where do I engage with the posthuman era? Thank you.

ROSI: Fantastic, yes. I'm so glad you asked, because this allows me to clarify my meta-methodological point. One thing about cartographies like the one I presented is that it's a way of surveying the field from a specific position. This means that the cartography expresses my perspective, so it is necessarily limited and partial. That partiality does not make it invalid; it makes it objective within the grounded parameters of my location. ———— This is why the feminist politics of location is a method I so strongly rely on. There's a whole tradition in feminist epistemology, on standpoint theory (Harding, 1991), and the importance of situated and partial perspectives (Haraway, 1988). My nomadic cartographies (Braidotti, 2011b) pertain to this tradition, which is a way of saying that I couldn't possibly be comprehensive. I couldn't, and I wouldn't want to. And I think the idea of cartographic renderings of a field of research is very important because then the dialogue between us would consist in comparing our respective cartographies. ———— I think that a cartographic method is a way of daring to take on the present. And I always take on the present as more on what we're in the process of becoming than what we're ceasing to be. But many of my colleagues are focusing more on what we're ceasing to be. As I said earlier, if you look at biopolitical scholarship, it's all about death and destruction, and what we're ceasing to be. So, it is actually necropolitical and it's extremely important, but we cannot do only that. ———— In terms of what "we" should do with East Asian studies, you've just given yourself a task. Draw that cartography and position the issues within it. What I know is that the Asian region as a whole is investing massively into transhumanism. Especially in Korea— the two journals, both the transhuman and posthuman journals, come out of Seoul. Korea is producing some of the most cutting-edge work on this. But it tends to stay very much within the Silicon Valley ideology—this is just a short term for the transhumanist delusion of downloading human consciousness into the computer. That's sort of summarizing a much more complex story. And there's much less critical posthumanism. There's a lot of interest, particularly emerging from Buddhist circles or critical Buddhism, reaching into Spinozism. Spinoza and Taoism work really well together. A lot of work happens in some regions in China, but I think you have to go to Korea, bits of Japan, and Singapore to see this happening.

AUDIENCE: In the context of cognitive capitalism, as you said, institutions are advancing to rethink those insufficiencies of earlier humanities, and are the ones that get funds. In other words, they are where capital and academia converge. So how do you think of this paradox? Are the people who are at the height of this hierarchy of capitalism, of inequality, the people who are now rethinking it? And do you think this could produce some sort of impartiality? Or that it can be acceptable as a phenomenon?

ROSI: The role of the universities in this is capital, literally. It's central. The university is us. And I happen to be profoundly in love with the university as an institution. Universities are centuries old. Bologna, the oldest we have in Europe, is 900 years old. And Coimbra is 700 years old. My little Utrecht is 365 years old. We've been there for a long time. And we've been training partially with difficulties, with exclusion, but we've been training young people through massive crises. We survived the introduction of the printing press. We almost survived the internet. It's a brilliant institution.

AUDIENCE: [*Laughter*]

ROSI: Why should an institution with such moral pedigree, with such energy, with such nobility in the heart take as its model the corporation—a fraudulent, bankrupt, dishonest, very recent institutional structure that actually hasn't gotten one thing right, certainly not since 2008? Why should that be the model and not us? ——— We've been training decent, discerning, creative, critical citizens for centuries. Now give us a break. We are the model. We need to remain the model for a twenty-first-century democracy of cognitive, critical, capitalizing citizens who can make a difference. That's our job. And if you look at the charter of the great university, Edinburgh, but Harvard also, essentially we are charities— with big endowments on the stock exchange, yes, but we're a public good. We are here to do things for the love of the world. That has to stay our central function. And I think that's why critical thinking can't just be negative and scoring points, and spreading nihilism, cynicism, and depression. ——— We need to energize. We need to give people a sense of the possible. We need to put the active back into activism. Thinking is really about dreaming possible scenarios. And only the university can do that. You people, your intelligence, vision, ambition. Even if we do our best, we are underemploying your resources massively, not because we don't know how to do it, but just because the means of cognitive access at your disposal are enormous. ——— Imagine that we actually activated everything that you're capable of doing and thinking. Imagine being Spinoza-*ized*, being potentiated to the nth power of what you're capable of doing. Just imagine—not in the Silicon Valley sense, merging with the machine, going singular, and running the globe, but in the sense of opening up to the possibilities that the world is giving you. Spinoza's definition of the ethical life is the affirmative opening up, taking in the world, taking it on, taking this convergence, shaping it in the direction of generosity, solidarity, fun, and making a livelihood. ——— How about saying capitalism is a really bad interpretation of the market economy? There are different forms of market economy that we could do. Commons-oriented. More shareable. Based on solidarity. That's really in the hearts of the millennials. Everything you stand for is sharing and not leaving anybody behind. Toward different forms of the market economy. ——— Why couldn't we use a university not just to apply the banality of what already is the case and is already ceasing to be, but also the university as dreaming up what we're in the process of becoming? We've done it so well in the past, it's needed now more than ever. So, universities.

AUDIENCE: [*Applause*]

JOHN: Let's end on that. For anyone interested in continuing the conversation, we have a session with Rosi tomorrow here in Gund Hall in the Stubbins room. If you can't find it, ask a tired architect who's walking around the building. We'll have an open forum to continue this conversation. Thanks very much to Rosi Braidotti.

References

Some ideas Rosi Braidotti presented in the lecture on which this book is based have been expanded in other publications she has published since. Those references are cited in the lecture text and listed here.

Ansell Pearson, Keith, and Protevi, John. 2016. "Naturalism in the Continental tradition." In: Kelly James Clark (ed.) *Blackwell Companion to Naturalism*. Oxford: John Wiley & Sons.

Asberg, Cecilia and Braidotti, Rosi. (eds.) 2018. A Feminist Companion to the Posthumanities. Cham: Springer International Publishing.

Barr, Marleen. 1987. *Alien to Femininity: Speculative Fiction and Feminist Theory*. New York: Greenwood.

Barr, Marlene. 1993. *Lost in Space. Probing Feminist Science Fiction and Beyond*. Chapel Hill: University of North Carolina Press.

Beck, Ulrich. 2007. "The Cosmopolitan condition: Why methodological nationalism fails." *Theory, Culture & Society*, 24(7/8): 286–90.

Bostrom, Nick. 2014. *Superintelligence: Paths, Dangers, Strategies*. Oxford: Oxford University Press.

Braidotti, Rosi, and Maria Hlavajova (eds.). 2018. Posthuman Glossary. London: Bloomsbury Academic.

Braidotti, Rosi, and Paul Gilroy (eds.). 2016. Contesting Humanities. London: Bloomsbury Academic.

Braidotti, Rosi, and Simone Bignall (eds.). 2018. Posthuman Ecologies. Rowman and Littlefield International.

Braidotti, Rosi, Emily Jones, and Goda Glumbyte (eds.). 2022. *More Posthuman Glossary*. London: Bloomsbury Academic.

Braidotti, Rosi. 1991. *Patterns of Dissonance: On Women in Contemporary French Philosophy*. Cambridge: Polity.

Braidotti, Rosi. 1994 and 2011a. *Nomadic Subjects: Embodiment and Sexual Difference in Contemporary Feminist Theory*. New York: Columbia University Press.

Braidotti, Rosi. 2002. *Metamorphoses: Towards a Materialist Theory of Becoming*. Cambridge: Polity Press.

Braidotti, Rosi. 2006. *Transpositions: On Nomadic Ethics*. Cambridge: Polity Press.

Braidotti, Rossi, ed. 2010. *The History of Continental Philosophy, Volume 7. After Poststructuralism: Transitions and Transformations*. Chicago: University of Chicago Press, 398.

Braidotti, Rosi. 2011b. *Nomadic Theory: The Portable Rosi Braidotti*. New York: Columbia University Press.

Braidotti, Rosi. 2013. *The Posthuman*. Cambridge: Polity.

Braidotti, Rosi. 2017. *Posthuman, All Too Human*. The 2017 Tanner Lectures on Human Values. Whitney Humanities Center, Yale University, and the Tanner Foundation.

Braidotti, Rosi. 2018. A theoretical framework for the critical posthumanities. *Theory, Culture & Society*, https://doi.org /10.1177/0263276418771486

Braidotti, Rosi. 2019. *Posthuman Knowledge*. Cambridge: Polity Press

Braidotti, Rosi. 2022. *Posthuman Feminism*. Cambridge: Polity Press.

Braidotti, Rosi. 2022. *More Posthuman Glossary*. London: Bloomsbury.

Clover, Joshua, and Julianna Spahr. 2014. *#Misanthropocene: 24 Theses*. Oakland, CA: Commune Editions.

Cooper, Melinda. 2008. *Life as Surplus: Biotechnology and Capitalism in the Neoliberal Era*. Seattle: University of Washington Press.

Creed, Barbara. 1993. *The Monstrous-Feminine. Film, Feminism, Psychoanalysis*. London: Routledge.

Crutzen, P. J., and E. F. Stoermer. 2000. "The Anthropocene." *Global Change Newsletter*, 41, 17–18.

Delanda, Manuel. 2016. *Assemblage Theory*. Edinburgh: Edinburgh University Press.

Deleuze, Gilles, and Felix Guattari. 1977. *Anti-Oedipus: Capitalism and Schizophrenia* I. New York: Viking Press.

Deleuze, Gilles, and Felix Guattari. 1987. *A Thousand Plateaus: Capitalism and Schizophrenia* II. Minneapolis: University of Minnesota Press.

Deleuze, Gilles. [1968] 1990. *Expressionism in Philosophy: Spinoza*. New York: Zone Books.

Deleuze, Gilles. [1970] 1988. *Spinoza: Practical Philosophy*. San Francisco: City Lights Books.

Deleuze, Gilles. 1993. *The Fold: Leibniz and the Baroque*. Minneapolis: University of Minnesota Press.

Deleuze, Gilles. 2003. *Pure Immanence: Essays on a Life*. New York: Zone Books.

Derrida, Jacques. 2008. *The Animal That Therefore I Am*. New York: Fordham University Press.

Epstein, Mikhail. 2012. *The Transformative Humanities: A Manifesto*. Translated and edited by Igor Klyukanov. New York: Bloomsbury.

Fanon, Frantz. 1967. *Black Skin, White Masks*. New York: Grove Press.

Ferrando, Francesca. 2013. "Posthumanism, transhumanism, antihumanism, metahumanism. and new materialism. Differences and relations." *Existenz. An International Journal in Philosophy, Religion, Politics and the Arts.* 8/2, 26–32.

Flannery, Tim. 1994. *The Future Eaters*. New York: Grove Press.

Foucault, Michel. 1977. *Discipline and Punish*. New York: Pantheon Books.

Foucault, Michel. 1978. *The Will to Knowledge. The History of Sexuality: 1*. London: Penguin Books.

Fukuyama, Francis. 2002. *Our Posthuman Future: Consequences of the Biotechnological Revolution*. London: Profile Books.

Gabrys, Jennifer. 2011. *Digital Rubbish: A Natural History of Electronics*. Ann Arbor: University of Michigan Press.

Gouges, de Olympe. 1791. *Declaration of the Rights of Woman and the Citizen*. https://www.bl.uk/collection-items /the-declaration-of-the-rights-of-woman-and-the-citizen

Grosz, E. 2011. "1. The Inhuman in the Humanities: Darwin and the Ends of Man." *Becoming Undone: Darwinian Reflections on Life, Politics, and Art*. Durham, NC: Duke University Press, 11–25.

Guattari, Felix. 1995. *Chaosmosis: An Ethico-aesthetic Paradigm*. Sydney: Power Publications.

Habermas, Jürgen. 2003. *The Future of Human Nature*. Cambridge: Polity Press.

Haraway, Donna. 1992. "The promises of monsters. A regen- erative politics for inappropriate/d others." In Lawrence Grossberg, Cary Nelson, and Paula Treichler (eds.). *Cultural Studies*. London: Routledge.

Haraway, Donna. 2016. *Staying with the Trouble: Making Kin in the Chthulucene.* Durham, NC: Duke University Press.

Haraway, Donna. 1988. "Situated Knowledges: The Science Question in Feminism as a Site of Discourse on the Privilege of Partial Perspective." *Feminist Studies*, vol. 14, no. 3: 575–55.

Harding, Sandra. 1991. *Whose Science? Whose Knowledge?* Ithaca, NY: Cornell University Press.

Hayles, Katherine N. 1990. *Chaos Bound: Orderly Disorder in Contemporary Literature and Science*. Ithaca, NY: Cornell University Press.

Hayles, Katherine N. 2005. *My Mother Was a Computer: Digital Subjects and Literary Texts*. Chicago, MI: University of Chicago Press.

Hayles, Katherine N. 2016. "Cognitive Assemblages: Technical Agency and Human Interactions." *Critical Inquiry*. 43 (1): 32–55.

Herbrechter, Stefan, 2013. *Posthumanism: A Critical Analysis*. London: Bloomsbury.

Irigaray, Luce. 1993. *An Ethics of Sexual Difference*. Ithaca, NY: Cornell University Press.

Kolbert, Elizabeth. 2014. *The Sixth Extinction*. New York: Henry Holt Company.

Kristeva, Julia. 1980. *Pouvoirs de l'horreur*. Paris: Editions du Seuil.

Kuokkanen, Rauna. 2017. "Indigenous epistemes." In Imre Szeman, Sarah Blacker, and Justin Sully (eds.). *A Companion to Critical and Cultural Theory*. London: John Wiley & Sons Ltd.

Kurzweil, Ray. 2006. *The Singularity is Near*. New York: Penguin Putnam.

Lorimer, Jamie. 2017. "The Anthropo-scene: A Guide for the Perplexed." *Social Studies of Science*: 47(1), 117–42.

Louverture, Toussaint. [1792] 2011. *Lettres à la France. Idées pour la Libération du people noir d'Haiti.* Bruyères-le-Chatel: Nouvelle Cité.

MacCormack, Patricia. 2014. *The Animal Catalyst*. London: Bloomsbury.

Macfarlane, Robert. 2016. "Generation Anthropocene: How humans have altered the planet forever." *The Guardian*, April 1. https://www.theguardian.com/books/2016/apr/01/generation-anthropocene-altered-planet-for-ever.

Moore, Jason. 2013. "Anthropocene, Capitalocene, and the myth of industrialization. World-Ecological Imaginations: Power and Production" in the Web of Life, June 16. https://jasonwmoore.wordpress.com/2013/06/16/anthropocene-capitalocene-the-myth-of-industrialization/>.

Moulier-Boutang, Yann. 2012. *Cognitive Capitalism*. Cambridge: Polity Press.

Nayar, Pramod K. 2013. *Posthumanism*. Cambridge: Polity Press.

New York Times Editorial Board. 2014. "Notes from the Plasticene epoch: From ocean to beach, tons of plastic pollution." *The New York Times*, June 15, SR10.

Papadopoulos, Dimitris. 2010. "Insurgent posthumanism." *Ephemera*, 10/2: 134–51.

Parikka, Jussi. 2015. *The Anthrobscene*, Minneapolis, MN: University of Minnesota Press.

Pepperell, Robert. 2003. *The posthuman manifesto*. Intellect Quarterly.

Pope Francis. 2015. *Encyclical Letter Laudato si': On Care for our Common Home*. Rome: The Vatican Press.

Rajan, Kaushik Sunder. 2006. *Biocapital: The Constitution of Postgenomic Life*. Durham, NC: Duke University Press.

Rich, Adrienne. 1984. "Notes toward a politics of location." In *Blood, Bread and Poetry*. New York: Norton.

Roden, David. 2014. *Posthuman Life: Philosophy at the Edge of the Human*. London: Routledge.

Rorty, Richard. 1998. *Achieving Our Country*. Cambridge, MA: Harvard University Press.

Rose, Deborah Bird. 2004. *Reports From a Wild Country*. Sydney: University of New South Wales Press.

Rose, Nikolas. 2007. *The Politics of Life Itself*. Princeton: Princeton University Press.

Said, Edward. 2004. *Humanism and Democratic Criticism*.
New York: Columbia University Press.

Schwab, Klaus. 2015. *The fourth industrial revolution*.
Foreign Affairs, December 12.

Scranton, Roy. 2015. *Learning to Die in the Anthropocene*.
San Francisco: City Lights Books.

Shiva, Vandana. 1997. *Biopiracy: The Plunder of Nature and
Knowledge*. Boston: South End Press.

Sloterdijk, Peter. 2009. "Rules for the Human Zoo: A response
to the Letter on Humanism." *Environment and Planning D:
Society and Space*, 27(1): 12–28.

Sterling, Bruce. 2012. *The Manifesto of Speculative Posthumanism*.
http://www.wired.com/2014/02/manifesto-speculative
-posthumanism/.

Stimpson, Catherine R. 2016. "The nomadic humanities."
Los Angeles Review of Books, July 12.

Todd, Zoe. 2015. "Indigenizing the Anthropocene." In Heather
Davis and Etienne Turpin (eds.). *Art in the Anthropocene:
Encounters Among Aesthetics, Politics, Environments
and Epistemologies*. London: Open Humanities Press,
241–54.

Tsing, Anna Lowenhaupt. 2015. *The Mushroom at the End of
the World: On the Possibility of Life in Capitalist Ruins*.
Princeton, NJ: Princeton University Press.

Viveiros de Castro, Eduardo. 2015. *The Relative Native: Essays on Indigenous Conceptual Worlds*. Chicago: HAU Press.

Wolfe, Cary. 2010. *What is Posthumanism?* Minneapolis, MN: University of Minnesota Press.

Wolfe, Cary. 2011. *Posthumanities*. Minneapolis, MN: University of Minnesota Press.

Contributors

Rosi Braidotti is a feminist continental philosopher and Distinguished University Professor Emerita at Utrecht University in the Netherlands. She holds degrees in philosophy from the ANU and the Sorbonne and honorary degrees from the University of Helsinki (2007) and Linköping University (2013). She is an Honorary Fellow of the Australian Academy of the Humanities (FAHA) and a member of the Academia Europaea. In 2022 she received the Humboldt Research Award for lifelong contribution to scholarship. Her main publications include *Nomadic Subjects* (2011) and *Nomadic Theory* (2011), *The Posthuman* (2013), *Posthuman Knowledge* (2019), *Posthuman Feminism* (2022), *The Posthuman Glossary* (2018), and *More Posthuman Glossary* (2022).

Colophon

Rosi Braidotti
Posthuman Knowledge and the Critical Posthumanities

Series editors: Ken Stewart and Marielle Suba
Editorial assistance: Carrie Bly
Proofreading: Mikhail Grinwald
Design: ELLA with Gabrielle Pulgar
Printing: Grafiche Veneziane, Italy

ISBN 978-3-95679-610-4

Distributed by The MIT Press, Art Data, Les presses du réel,
and Idea Books

Every effort has been made to contact the rightful owners with
regard to copyrights and permissions. We apologize for any
inadvertent errors or omissions.

Published by
Harvard Design Press   Sternberg Press
48 Quincy Street   71–75 Shelton Street
Cambridge, MA 02138   UK–London WC2H 9JQ
gsd.harvard.edu   www.sternberg-press.com

Harvard Design Press is the book imprint of the Harvard
University Graduate School of Design.

The Incidents

The Architecture of Taste
Pierre Hermé

Freedom of Use
Anne Lacaton and Jean-Philippe Vassal

Abstract from the Concrete
David Harvey

Architectural Ethnography
Atelier Bow-Wow

Design Thinking in the Digital Age
Peter G. Rowe

"Insert Complicated Title Here"
Virgil Abloh

Beyond the Collaboration
Sterling Ruby and Raf Simons

Design in a Frame of Emotion
Hannah Beachler with Jacqueline Stewart and Toni L. Griffin

Inhabiting the Negative Space
Jenny Odell

A Rage in Harlem: June Jordan and Architecture
Nikil Saval

Democracy and Urban Form
Richard Sennett